CW01426213

Coloured Truths

Coloured Truths

By

Francesca Hunt

First Published in 2024
by Henwtra Publishing

Copyright © Francesca Hunt 2024

Several of these poems have appeared in Reach
Magazine, Writers' Forum, Online publications, teaching
material and in anthologies.

The moral right of the author has been asserted.

This book is sold subject to the condition that no part of
it shall be reproduced, stored in a retrieval system (other
than for the purposes of review), or transmitted in any
form or by any means, electronic, mechanical,
photocopying, recording or otherwise, without the prior
permission in writing of the copyright owner.

ISBN: 978-1-4457-5961-6
Imprint: Lulu.com

Dedication: to my husband, Philip.

Author's Note

My thanks to all who have catalysed and fed my love for Poetry, in particular close family and friends, but also poets: Alison Chisholm, Jim Bennett and Cahal Dallat who have gently pushed and pulled me up the learning curve towards the vast open field…

"Go inwards. Find your inner space, and suddenly, you will find an explosion of light, of beauty, of ecstasy – as if suddenly thousands of roses have blossomed within you and you are full of their fragrance." — Osho

List of Poems:

Travelled Suitcases

Once the teacups and matching side-plates
are washed and returned to her china-cabinet,
I lift one of the suitcases onto the table.
My eyes catch the grandfather clock, 4.30pm.

Her front room, the lounge, with sashed bay windows
onto the avenue, rose-petal carpet and velvet drapes
will lose summer's enticing light before I'm free
from the daily task, a diligent great-niece's duty

when visiting her aged aunt. Today, it's Case 2.
I accept Kendal mint-cake from a crystal jar, smile
as I divert my gaze from sparrows enjoying blue sky.
Her swollen-jointed hands move the clasps – Click.

Just like the other five, this is filled to overspill
with yellow Kodak and blue-white Ilford folders
of black-and-white prints, many with serrated borders
no more than two inches by one; also individual framed

portraits denoting occasions, old metal tins,
the sort that carried Christmas toffees,
now promoted to hold her negative strips –
all to greet my youthful eyes. Her face, the softest,

roundest with warm-hugging smile
as she tells me who everyone is – names
I heard last year on pictures I will see again next year…
When can I pretend to need the bathroom? Not yet.

Now I lean to dust those suitcases.
They lie in my attic, unopened for fifty years
with family heirlooms, treasures and knick-knacks.
The clasps still click the same.

Foreign

Queen Anne's dance of summer lace,
with dotted blood-red pricks,
umbrellas Ox-Eye Daisies
and the uncoil of sleep-tight ferns.

A blackbird's song syncopates
to the click of my footsteps
on dawn's dew-swept road.
I stop, caught by reflected light.

Under breeze-quiver Dock leaves
lie a comb, coke-can, and hat.
The Aluminium electrolysed from Bauxite,
Polythene, Polyester, synthesised from oil –

the autumn foliage is digested with decorum,
as urban invasion chokes spring shoots.

Sitting by the Log Burner as January Marches

Edging to longer days, I'm surrounded
by youth's stuff, much of it not used
for years, I settle into mellow vintage,
like a new Beaujolais still corked
but promising good things at a later date.

Some say indulgent lounging should be fought
before it catalyses decline. The new year
heralded resolutions – calorie counting,
walking, perhaps the thousand-mile challenge,
and Cadair Idris, before autumn's out.

But the call of words to craft images
invades, possesses, demands to flow
graphite across virgin bleached paper
in my new moleskin notebook.
No rush, I'll enjoy a comfort-nap first.

Fourteen Pounds a Kilo

Do you see the new-born snuggled
close to mother's wool against winter's
frost-bitten, furrowed fields?

Do you smile at youthful play,
the scamper over discarded tractor tyres,
the shudder of udders as mouths suckle?

Do you enjoy the air-lifting tones,
the call of an ewe, and reply of her lamb
across two acres of freedom?

Do you grow fresh mint or buy the sauce,
and roast a butcher-packaged leg,
bloodless, for Sunday lunch after church?

Do you taste the fear
of lambs taken
for humane slaughter?

Do you hear the night-long howls
of the mothers
through your bedroom window?

Two Paths Converge.
(after Robert Frost)

I come from both, alone.
Two of me walk –
the seen, the persona,
but also, the silent, latent me.

Two rivers converge.
One carries silt,
the strength of earth.
The other reflects the moon.

Portal

Hinges are rusted shut.
I peer through iron bars
to sunshine speckled grass.
Shakespeare sits writing sonnets.

A squirt of WD40 –
I enter.
Where have all the poets gone?

The Powder Room

Standing proud on its pedestal,
a Belfast of breeding berates the builders –
Why not hang the mirror opposite
to reflect this porcelain beauty?

With verdigris joints, taps knock in disdain.
The eighties octagonal mirror ponders
the fuss: nothing to get steamed-up about…
it sees dentures and toothpaste, fingers squashing spots

and razors flicking stubble every day.
It relishes guests, who peep behind cupboard doors.
Then… there are the beauties who shed clothes
to bathe – Wow, virtual images worth a stare.

Standing on claw-feet, cast iron with chips of age,
the laid-back bath enjoys a soak, a gentle caress,
a scour to remove the itch from human debris –
abandoned skin and black bits from between toes.

The loo, bristling with pseudonyms,
toilet, lavatory, water-closet, latrine,
privy or bog – depending upon its social status,
is an individual of few words.

Its down to earth nature is admired
by all who read upon its throne. It takes
what's coming with a flush of excitement,
and only requests a blindfold, brush and bleach.

The bidet, confused and redundant, installed
for snob value, watches, waiting
for the occasional gardener's foot –
it has long since forgotten its bathroom role.

Ben Hadem
(After: 'Abou Ben Adhem' by Leigh Hunt)

Ben awoke from a dream
to a room, cupped with moonlight like a lily.
There an angel sat, her smile a beam,
her wings snow white and frilly.

Words flew from her quill of gold
as a whisper caressing his book.
Ben – now awake and sat up bold,
leant over to take a look.

Hey... what yer doing?
That's me Math's homework
and me pen yer chewing,
I'm going to look a right jerk.

She raised her head,
I'm writing names of those precious to you.
Ben grabbed the page to read.
You've got it wrong – it's Man City, not Man U.

Englynion

Freedom

they sail out dark to sea   the slow tide turns
no bat nor bird nor tree
spirit awakes   sprite can see
float in freedom   fire lifts me

sounds of sixties

raging fire broke those nights   rags from bodies
hit the sky   high as kites
bags packed   bogus pace of frights
he died of hidden delights

New Messages

anger drums my head I grab his mobile
lust-fed cheat   lost sheet-cred
burps and belches bound for bed
untethered   no text unread

Journey to Tuonella.

She watched his boat set sail, day after day,
pristine, blue paint against the surf
only to return at night, fewer fish each time.

'The tide is wrong,'
he would say, 'weather is changing,
the sea doesn't carry fish like it used to.'

Each night they'd watch the lighthouse arc
sweeping across ancient smuggler caves;
forgotten loot buried deep within the crags.

A white swan, wings stretched from shadows,
rose with cor anglais plaintive voice
to carry lamentation to his winter's sky.

Thirteen James Street

Whitewash reflected a solitary streetlight,
thick, thick walls, a solid buttress to mountain gales
whipping from the Carneddi, rattling tiles
on sweat-built miners' homes. We arrived

and scrambled round the back, mud, squelch,
the hoot of owls. Next-door shared cheese
and Jacob's Crackers, from a bright orange packet,
as they talked in funny accents, using foreign words.

Wrapped in blankets on a flagstone floor,
I listened to snores and the scrunch of a mouse.
The camping kettle whistled, steaming hot tea,
removal vans crawled up the pot-holed lane. Toys, toys

and fresh clean clothes – it would be school
next week. Squashed in a galvanised tub, I'm first
in the queue for Sunday's scrub. Cold concrete –
I missed the old home's toe-tickling carpet

and proper white bath. Depressive debris,
the grey-slate tips glinted purple, darkened
by Welsh rain – a perfect playground
for me and my brothers and Tim, our dog.

Snow-crusted peaks through misty murk,
transient light's haunting shadows lit my artist's blood.
Time, distance, separation left a silent vacuum,
homeland called my name. I came back, I came back.

Proserpina (after: 'Proserpina' by Dante Gabriel Rossetti)

I dig ivy roots from allotment clay
as leaves shrivel under glyphosate.

Seeds of the loin land on barren soil,
Eve, cursed by poisoned pomegranate seed

toils the winter months in underground
darkness, as Dante obsesses, capturing

her transient beauty on canvas
and in sonnet. Her blood leaches

to earth, as I thrust my spade
deep into his malignant delusion.

12

Still Birth.

(after: Dali's 'Archaeological Reminisces of Millet's Angelicus')

December icicles hang from the picture rail
with faded paintings of summer daisies.
Teeth are cleaned once, and once again to remove
the sweet remnants of dinner's tiramisu.

She clothes herself in thick winceyette
buttoned to the neck, light off, inched
to her edge. Football finished, six-pack
downed, burping, he staggers out.

The nightly ritual finds both relieved to escape
the black cloud hanging on five-amp cable
where once there was light and laughter.
A stone monument, bent, desiccated,

cowering in empty prayer, she mourns
her vacated womb, barren to future seed.
No child cries from the dusty crib,
no wide-eyed gurgles framed by golden

curls. Neon, flashing red against black sky,
eats his loins – cheap at twice the price,
until his stoned statue of guilt climbs
back in with icicles wrapped in winceyette.

Poetry without words
(After: Turner's 'Snow Storm Steamboat off a Harbour's Mount')

Indistinct swathes merge
browns, oranges, cream

with a touch of blue.
Close up – nothing,

like a dictionary of words spilt
randomly under a book title.

Stand back – scrabble squares
align, words flow to tell a story,

each brush mark, each colour,
speaks beyond their placement and hue.

Tanka

walking through bluebells
branches crackle underfoot
a broken promise
as machines spray herbicide
on our ever-giving earth

Virtual Image, Real Truth

I've given up searching
in the mirror for beauty.
They say it's hidden inside.
I removed the silver backing,
still no sign of me.

Then it occurred to me, if I reflect
the mirror in a mirror
I may catch
a virtual of the virtual me.
But do two virtuals add to real?

I banished the mirror from the bedroom,
avoided blackened shop-windows,
and kept my eyes peeled forward
on life's clear path
ahead... not searching for my beauty.

Then, I saw it...
Me. I was inside, inside everything...
the trees, the ground... the earth
the sky and in this body
which is often called Me.

Night Intrusion

Magic awakes on the chime of midnight.
Braced against darkness, wrapped in a red scarf,
flask under arm, I stand and breathe the silence
where time is still; that other world of no people.

A shadow hoots from the barn, its black eyes
camouflaged from prey. The breeze of its wake
tingles my cheek as it dives for a mouse
scurrying in undergrowth lit by my torch.

A two-thirds moon, coy behind cloud, blushes
amber-red. Venus chats millions of miles away.
I stand as a dot, significant in my head,
but a nano-needle in the eternal pine-forest.

A mallard and his slumbersome lady lift heads
from wings, fearful of unexpected intrusion.
My snow-heavy boots crack twigs on winter's ice,
a prelude to spring's swooping buzzards.

Absent: Glenys Jones

At the seventh tip at seven-thirty,
morning workmen watched
the slip of slurry;
slow at first
but gathering momentum.

From my bedroom window, I saw
friends wave and kiss parents *goodbye*.
Teacher rang the brass bell; the ordered
lines went inside for registration.
Then it happened...

yells, cracks,
a torrential roar –
too fast, too strong,
a sea of black,
flattened – they were gone – buried.

sirens shattered morbid silence; frozen,
voiceless screams, people wrenched
at earth, heedless of danger,
dragging boulders and beams,
searching, listening.

Mam didn't want more trouble
from the Social. She kept me from school
that day because of my bruises.
I wish I had gone –
My silence isn't like theirs.

(21st October 1966, slurry from tip seven on the hill above Pant Glas Primary school, Aberfan, Glamorgan, flattens the school killing 116 children and 28 adults.)

I am

I am the New Year's reveller,
planning a decade of dreams,
pictures to paint, paths to walk,
retirement stretches with money to spend.

I am your anonymous victim, the person
in your wake, as you coughed without care.
Spring unfolds with a hope I cannot share
alone in a sterile, bustling prison.

I am the statistic under a ventilator,
Nurses dressed like spacemen voice comfort.
Excluded family hold red roses
to the window. You stole my breath.

Sight

Did you want to see what he left behind
as his footsteps fade into an angry future
and his memory stagnates in the minds
of those who only see with eyes?

Did you want to see what he made
as truth the day he wrote those words
to you in his locked journal buried
in the attic before he wrote his Will?

Did you want to see the enormity
of his gift to life before his illness struck
those days when you were far away
not interested in his actions or thoughts?

Did you want to see the colour of his heart
the rhythm of his beat before he left
and was buried in an unmarked
grave abroad in foreign soil?

Did you want to see his hungry childhood
his parents begging for food on prewar streets
parents who later welcomed occupation
becoming wretched sub-people yet again?

I Run the Bumps of a Dinosaur's Tongue...

through purple oaks
to a wicker nest
where eagles invite
me to stop for tea.

Dead mice taste
fine when seasoned,
battered and dunked
in barbecue sauce.

Northerly gusts
drop
me

to yellow waters
where mother
lies bathing,

drinking crème de menthe
from a crystal glass
as mermaids paint her nails green.

I jostle angry ants,
pull the plug
and crawl away.

Moonshine and Cheese

The amber moon's
beckoning eyes sparkle
through miles of silence.

Palms support my chin.
I ponder,
Is it really made of cheese?

Through the open window, I tiptoe
up ladder rungs. Snowball-clouds
snuggle me across jet sky.

I choose my wine, salivating;
sweet Sauternes suits Stilton,
and chambré Burgundy for Cheddar.

The creamy texture crumbles
to my fork, my mouth opens wide,
ready to bite its creamy welcome...

... in March 2014

(After: Edward Hopper, Cape Cod Morning, 1950,
and Health issue, interwoven)

low morning light, a yellow wash of hope,
early sunshine peeped over the Carneddau
to play on green oak buds bursting promise

Noise, a thud, a churn of tractor tyres
on pot-holed lanes, a distant gull echoes the sea
Of course, I knew, I didn't need confirmation, I knew

The dog, one ear alert cocked in readiness,
three years ago, the master left a scribbled note
under the pepper mill, *devastated, prognosis poor*

he would return but only afterwards..
part of me thought this glow, this morning kiss,
just may trumpet hope. If only she had spoken

that night, conveyed understanding,
I took those moments alone, fed on gold,
disowning pyrites, today would be the start...

Letters leach through the letter box,
the oncologist's all-clear
there won't be one from him.

Self Portrait, Signed — Le Pinceau

I step from palette to easel
carrying pigment,
and climb to white canvas,
freshly gessoed, primed for use.

The brief – paint a self-portrait;
but there's no mirror.
Perhaps I don't need it;
a photo likeness would catch

a superficial me, each hair
to perfection. You could trace DNA
back to the hog that proudly wore
my bristles. The Master said *go deep,*

explore inside. If I break
the steel that holds my hairs…
I can't without pliers –
none were mentioned in his brief.

So… I'll do my own thing
It'll be all about me, the inside me.
I slosh ultramarine
not at the top, I'm not sky,

terre-verte here on the left
rose madder for the sea
burnt umber to the middle.
Then I'll layer it, with metaphor —

a cadmium boat with tapered oars
sails the linseed sea, a play of titanium
against ochre, a crescendo of phalo
dies to umber cadence.

Time to rest my bristles in turps,
the portrait done, genuine
Pre-Raphaelite brush-hood
painted for my Master.

One's Upbringing

Framed by a spirit-levelled fence,
stand rows of regimented beans
planted at textbook separation,
anxiety fed, striving to please.

Sown by nature's wave, red campion
mingle with violets in a polka-dot meadow.
Sun-kissed buttercups laugh, a plateau
of cow parsley dances the breeze.

Missing Daisy

(After: Monet's 'Bathers at La Grenouillère' 1869, Édouard Manet:
Déjeuner sur l'Herbe 1863)

'You didn't tell me Daisy wasn't coming
and I've baked her special cake,
the one with chocolate butter icing
splitting layers of vanilla sponge.'

'After hand-hidden sniggers and whispers,
following Manet's stream-side picnic
dans le jardin, sur l'herbe, her father forbade
attendance – not the place for ladies to be seen.'

'Pity, Daisy always brings the rugs.
My yellow satin frock's back from cleaners',
now there's nowhere fit to sit,
and the caterers prepared for twelve.'

'Hasten, the champers is chambré-ing,
no longer cerulean-ice chilled;
crockery and cutlery are missing,
and the hound wishes to partake of cake.'

'Shut-it Quentin; you were in charge
of details. All I've brought
is the cake, iPhone for footie results,
nothing else, not even my swimsuit.'

With stilted répartie, a soupçon of camaraderie
lubricated by ethanol and cake, the Punch satire
degrades to Blackpool postcard bosoms.
The dog scoffs leftovers, they, dormant dans le soleil.

Truth Colours Window Glass

Newlywed, he peers to red roses,
lip-edges fading to softer pink,
fledgling disagreements crawling
unseen like spiders into corners.

Career-ladder man, twenty-something,
sees green leaves, kids, Domestos,
Victoria Sponge and homemade candles.
I fill bins and iron tomorrow's shirt.

Brown cracks of middle-age,
my arms sag like cutting scythes,
my makeup brash under greying sky,
gone is the white canvas of wedding,

He sees black tar bubbling,
pot-holes beneath my window.
Next door's buxom blossom
invites, crumpet served, blue ice.

Three score and ten, through clear panes,
love-blushed by my cream-cake waist
and frumpy pyjamas, his smile lights
the log-burner as we share a purple snug-rug.

I pull the curtains tight,
tight closed now, as night draws in.
An old man's glasses magnify.
Today he sees me, his wife.

a cheek full of tongue… erratum

Life isn't bobbing up and down
on carousel horses
or racing off with Mary Poppins
to dance London roofs with sweeps.

Life isn't oysters cheering escape from walrus teeth
on a beach under Saharan sun, nor owl and cat
on a pea-green boat, calling 999 SOS rescue
to lifeboatmen in orange suits and black boots.

Life isn't backward travel, tears
before finger prick, a Hatter tea-party
without jam today, or preparing for battle
before sunset cracks the looking-glass to shards.

Life isn't magic wardrobes, with panels
to Narnia, or dancing yellow-brick roads
with lions, straw men and rusty metal,
chasing rainbows to nowhere dreams.

Life is a serious business, 1,2,3
alpha to omega, in any language you please,
syntax correct, blue-black ink, blotted
with pink absorbent, each letter elegantly formed.

Life is rules, from birth to grave…
you cry when your bum is slapped,
you don't cry when you're bullied
you cry when the movie is sad,
but stiff upper lip at a loved one's funeral.

Life is a fishing rod primed with bait
lowered into your pool. Take a bite.
You're pulled out for inspection
then chucked back to the sharks. Repeat.

Life is not fun, you're not meant to smile
laugh or yell with ecstasy. The world loves
sadness, the woes of folk comparing ill health,
arguing who's closest to the grave.

Erratum
Erratum…
kindly replace all affirmatives
with negation and vice versa.

Harps Stand Silent at my Feet

I catch the 16:52
between the rain and snow

and scramble ladder-rungs,
steeples to the sky
through yellow gorse prickles

my pillows absorb torrents of fever
family mop me with sponges and towels
as mother prays

a diminuendo   a rallentando
I'm attached to a saline drip   drip
09:45   it's doctors and blood pressure

instruments click and tick and hic
up   as green phosphor waves swim
on the silent scream   the 3.05 is early

time passes without measure
faces come   smiles go   Platform 1
19:54   Lacrimosa in D minor

notes hang on the metal bed-frame
with scythe ever ready
he shadows Platform 4

but I return to tungsten light
on the 07:43 Euston express
from a vacuous tunnel

a cacophony of bells herald
family-goo   their hugs imprison me
in welcome home   *halleiujah*

his harvest not reaped
I catch his grim scowl
he departs on the 14.44

I Prefer Disorder

Early evening, sunset glows,
blackbirds call their last song.
A hearty dinner, worries vanish
as I breathe your perfumed rose.

They say today gives tomorrow, but
Chaos theory's double-rod pendulum
dances a random jig,
today's present does not give future

When edges of time turn rust-purple
and blackbirds flee pi r-squared,
eat your pop eyed greens,
spinach grows straighter toes.

Toothache will vanish
as red arrows paint the sky
and the mayor buys roses,
two a penny, at Covent Garden.

We Soft Embrace

We soft embrace.
Fire tangos through our bodies
coupled as coiled pythons,
in flagrante delicto.
Cayenne stirs the gossip cauldron.

Time's pendulum slows,
as summer heat fades.
We throw high voltage plates
across a blood of thorns.
Explosive photons strangle
exhaled air

Memories of vows, spoken to loves,
creep back as wheat husks are cleared.
Autumn winds blow; the red rose dies
to winter snow. We seal our hunger
one last time, in soft embrace.

Dent de Lion

To taste forbidden love,
yellow flowers, summer's sun-kissed
blush of youth   he loves me…
he loves me not…

Fizzy Corona-pop gulped on a school trip,
purple-brown nectar, sugar rich –
Burdock fuels the group singsong,
he loves me.

Ice-seed, crystal tears,
silk-worm wisps and dead stalks
are trapped in a paperweight bell-jar,
he loves me not.

By eating Dandelion leaves for thirty days
Theseus draws strength to defeat
the half-man, half-bull, Minotaur,
he loves me.

Weeds on a neighbour's nurtured lawn,
are attacked at dawn with glyphosate.
Shrivelled debris remain, his stature stolen,
he loves me not.

I sip forgotten warmth from a mug
of caffeine-free ground roots
as winter sun dips below the horizon,
he loves me.

No Stick – Just Carrot

The private life of a carrot,
be it yellow, orange or blue,
is secret and elaborate,
and quite unbelievably true.

He lives, unlike a parrot,
underground in an earthy hole,
his choice of friend, deliberate,
is the sweet and cuddly mole.

His favourite food is the faggot,
which he rarely gets to eat,
washed down with a glass of claret –
what a heavenly treat.

He oozes healthy carotene
with vitamins B and K.
His silky skin, like velveteen,
diffuses a light bouquet.

With very little dosh to spend,
he needs a nine-carat ring,
so he can wed his lady friend,
in hat and tails, next spring.

Women Drivers?

As soon as Dad revved
and went down a gear
I knew it was time to shut my eyes
and whisper a few Hail Marys
in my spaghetti-churned mind.

I didn't want to die yet,
I'd hardly started living,
It was all school and homework;
I had plans –
marry– definitely, kids? Maybe.

Once I'd heard
the Doppler lowered frequency
of oncoming… passing horn,
as Dad swerved back into lane,
his breathing returned to normal…

I could release my car-seat grip
for now.
I just might make it to sweet-sixteen
and get a boyfriend
like Liesl in *The Sound of Music*…

Today I grip my seat
but smile
as hubby corners fast
on the tail of a blue Fiat 500
ranting at women drivers.

Dragon's Blood: Hiraeth...

Mist whispers a dance to the haunted song
of snow-wrapped hills. My feet crunch
autumn's bracken, mirroring footsteps trudged
by men wheezing through silica lungs,
as they crocodile to work with the rising sun.

Slate caverns echo history's cries: warriors
trampled by Edward, that man of castles
with no soul for the tongue of butchered
Celts. Laments bellow through the valleys
as dragons roar blood on rugby fields.

Father, always Today not Tomorrow

A big man, he was six-foot-three,
cheese-and-wine expanded girth,
temper to match his red-dyed hair,
and nouse to bull-doze opposition.

'My name is Jack, so call me Jack,'
was Father's instruction to my fiancé.
I wasn't allowed to call him *Dad* or *Father,*
his logic – 'I don't call you Daughter.'

True to his Leo star-sign, he ate cowards
for breakfast but purred like a pampered puss
when his ego was polished; compliments
were candy floss to fortify his halo.

His moustache was sometimes a Kaiser-twirl,
shaped into a handlebar with homemade wax,
or an Adolf toothbrush-bristle. His vanity
admired both in blackened shop windows.

On a high, he squandered housekeeping
on sixties-cool pink shirts and sheepskin.
On a low, weeks of pyjamas and stale bread,
we watched the line of fungus coffee mugs grow.

At night he'd compose sonatas, us kids
barely dared to flush the toilet, eat or breathe.
Then, as by magic, a switch would change...
he'd spit and polish to wall-booming Wagner.

On days smiling infinite summer sun,
he'd shout, 'boots on, where's the dog lead?'
In red and green anoraks, with sandwiches,
a flask of tea, we'd stride off into the Carneddau.

Back at dusk, with blisters and grazed knees,
charged by yells, chatter and soul, we'd queue
for baths, one in, one out, water colder and grubbier;
then collapse to white sheets. Tomorrow, who knows?

Moon Glass

Silver ghost, mysterious orb
shimmering in blackness of sea,
a keeper of childhood prayers
since Eve first walked the soil,

a constant friend, a part of earth,
but separate. On sleepless nights
I long to reach out and touch you
as we churn human soul-pain together.

Armstrong visited– *One small step
for man, one giant leap for mankind,*
but I wouldn't want to crush the shell
and break your spell of milky-pearl.

I sit, palms under chin, and stare
to space. Forget centripetal force,
gravitation, orbit speed and radius,
to me, you're Stilton for my Rosé.

A call to make

Volcanic upthrust, unseen
tectonic plates grind and growl,
they churn buried regrets –
that phone call I have not made.

Walkers kick Basalt rocks,
Uranium-dated to Earth's birth,
your ancient crags rise with wisdom
from haunted shores of Llyn Cau.

Sit silent, majestic Cadair
your peak staring through mist
of time, your body clothed in grit,
grass and wind-stumped trees.

As clouds rise and evening sun paints
your glacial-cut chair purple, I smile,
pick up my rucksack and hurry…
to network coverage, I have a call to make…

Stolen

Porth Neigwl calls, calls me back
through narrow lanes, and dappled gorse;
but there's no Mr. Whippy,
no chocolate sauce to sticky my wrinkled hand.

Barbed wire suffocates.
I cannot yell and run free-fall
through vastness of talc-dust sand-dunes.
Keep Out notices restrict me

to a planked pathway,
dog-waste bins steal the wild.
Gone is the splat of glistening jelly-fish
reflecting evening orange.

Kids' voices no longer rise above
white dragon roar. Single-use bottles
bob in detergent scum, Big-Mac cartons
punctuate *progress* infested sands.

Clouds crystallise,
knives cut summer's blue sky
to paper shreds, confetti memories
trodden by hob-nail boots.

Eirlys — The Snow Lily

A single drop of solitude nestles in last year's uncut
thicket, it stands like a fledgling swallow that missed
autumn's call to migrate.

Cars bumble the soft-verge lane, tainting snow-white
petals with tractor scattered mud, the lone flower bows
and bobs green-dabbed milk to the breeze.

I could snap its stalk, give it sterile water on a
window-ledge where it can peer to open landscape
through pungent air of bleach, polish and discordant
voices.

No, this fair maid of February, with arching bell and
leather-green leaves, stands defiant, unscarred by the
thrust from sugar-store bulb, through frozen earth to
greet the sky – she must be first to salute and open a
New-Year's curtain to sun-stretched days.

Brifo

Sadness hurting me terrible
I an' seen like of it b'fore,
yest'day it was, morning,
aafpass sem, they say.

Now jest seen husband
talking to parch he was,
on doorstep,
her being proper religious,
Chapel everee Sunday.

My butty she were
proper chopsy
go everee where we did,
enjoyed a joke like schoolgirls,
plenty of clecs and cwtch.

She took real bad,
with pneumonia it was,
gone now.
Were more nicer than me.
Always had good words.

(Brifo…. (pronounced Brivo) = hurting, Parch = minister)
(butty = friend, chopsy = talkative, clecs = gossip, cwtch = cuddles/hugs
Poem written in Wenglish… the dialect of South Wales valleys. The verb
often appears at the end of the sentence e.g. 'it was', mimicking frequent
use in Welsh language)

take a read

from red front cover
to closing page

a mountain range
valley to peak to valley

from top left down
meander across

miles between gorse
hedges and insects for birds

eyes journey
to bottom right

river flows to horizon
chapter to chapter

lines leap like salmon upstream
to red back cover

Black Horse of Lloyd's Bank

Tryg, a drover's dog from Sarn Meillteyrn
slips his collar at night to chase sheep.
Death sentence passed, execution planned,
Tryg bolts to freedom when backs are turned.

The animals are shod for the miles ahead.
Geese are walked through warm pitch,
onto fine gravel and finally cold water
to solidify their stone-coated feet.

Blacksmiths nail horseshoes onto cattle hooves.
Hierarchy amongst beasts is settled by skirmish
as they wait in Cae Blaenau pens
for the drovers to finish with beer and women folk.

The men in wide brimmed hats, their bodies
wrapped in waxed paper to insulate and shield
from rain, dressed in smocks, long coats,
knee-length woolen socks and clogs,

walk the route they've trod for years:
Llanfair, Pont Scethin, Bwlch Y Rhiwgyr
to Bont Ddu, Dolgellau, Welshpool to London.
A highwayman emerges from dense oak,

Pit-bull at his side. *'Your valuables or life.'*
The master recognises Tryg and shouts,
Seize . Caught by the neck,
the bandit's blood taints slate and quartz.

With soft soap, rich in sheep fat, rubbed on soles
of socks, they journey cairn-marked mountain ways,
stopping at rivers for water, inns for liquor,
food and rest, with ha'penny fields for animals.

In London markets, sale money
is exchanged for 'promises' – theft-proof notes
issued to be cashed by the account holder
on return home, in Drovers 'Black Horse Bank,

run by the Lloyd family at Dolbran.
They promise:
'To pay the Bearer the sum of .... on Demand.'
Tryg enjoys his reprieve in a tighter fitting collar.

Cwm Ffynnon Caseg

Dressed in childhood sunshine and red anorak
my small feet scramble history's forgotten grandeur,
Carneddau — vast home of ancient spirits

locked in jagged granite spikes. Dragons' teeth
of Yr Ellen's ridge bite the sky, sheep tracks
rise to horizon – a black line cut against fogged

purple, brackened mountains, punctuated
by rusted war-fragments, torn wings and wheels
and the century-old rubble from workers' hafods.

I stand by Llyn Caseg, caught in waft and whisper
of waist-high reeds, sun-tipped as grey-cream
light filters through snow-melt fish-rippled water

to highlight rocks, blue, bronze and moss-green.
A place where horses birth and die,
a place where death roams and locals fear.

In years to come, I will be brought back,
but I will not see the purple-grey crag
bathed in September's gold.

Aberdaron

a touch of feather
as moon-gloss wrinkles sea
dark shadows swallow night
to flute of song

pink blossom trickles
to seagulls howl
an electric milk cart
clicks the pilgrim path

my breath held
shadows lean
from gravestones
centuries look out to sea

I will not hear the wind-howl
nor metal echo round the cwm
I will dance free

A Child's Christmas in Red Boots

Watch me
in my Christmas red boots
play with bucket and spade,
not gritty sand but snow
as pure and white
as Santa's beard.

Listen, I laugh
with the robin who digs,
chasing worms
below the cold
as Mum cooks the turkey
and Dad stokes the fire.

Hear my song
as I wash hands and nails
clean, ready for Jesus'
birthday meal.
I bow my head
as Grandad says Grace.

Look as I kiss
the snowman's carrot nose,
and wrap a wool scarf
round his neck
to keep him as cosy
as my feet in Santa's red boots.

Come spring, come summer
my boots, cobwebbed-red,
sit by the back door... waiting
waiting until the snow magic
starts falling again,
white and thick   I'm ready...

Yellow Formica in my Life

A pattern of grasses and autumnal seed
clambers across the sunburst Formica table
in the center of our dining room.
Six matching chairs, six chatter and eat.

Beatles croon 'Yeah, Yeah, Yeah',
the Berlin Wall rises, segregating
families, east and west.
We children build Lego houses on the table
as the kids next door speak Welsh.

Nuclear protestors storm London,
train robbers scoop 2.6 million,
and President JFK is shot in Dallas –
but the Beatles and Dewi from next door,
just wanna hold my hand.

Our parents squabble — it's DR NO
not 'Love me do', the big freeze of '63,
in our igloo home, the air's cut by ice pick.
Six people eat a silent lunch at the table.
as a chimp called Ham shoots to space.

After a plateau of debt and niggles,
a hot-iron hole in the cheery Formica,
Dad scores his winning goal,
a new job, finances secure, smiles.
over Shepherd's Pie and sparkling Shlöer.

Now, sixty years later
with a reconditioned sunburst top
and cobalt-blue legs, my childhood
table stands defiant next to my easel.
I paint, inspired by time-carved memories.

Breakfast at Blaenau – I remember...

bread and jam, Grandma's best china
lazy summer days of childhood fun
all wrapped in honey-sweet magenta,
easy times, floating under rosebud spell
no pressure to conform or rebel   until
after tea that day,
                        blue flashing cars and
uniform police come to caution Grandpa

for helping himself, forgetting to pay,
for pretending the innocence of lamb.
'Easy at my age, thought I'd paid a fiver,
so sorry, won't happen again, I'll leave
them a tip.'   He's off to the *Harp*, soda
in gin, lemon for colour, drink after drink –
'no good'll come of it', he'll be singing, off
into the night, pinching souvenir trinkets, a'
offering for Grandma.
                   Bacon, egg and beans
gild memories of Grandpa's fresh start!

Purrfect Address

painted red lips
a plastic blow-up
doll creaks
in skylight breeze

tethered on string
tied to his bed-post
next to historic
conquest notches

flat deflated
his ego burst
as memory fades
he doesn't speak

through the open window
a Tabby visits
soft fur to arthritic fingers
milk in saucer

tea and cornflakes
he'll go out shopping
Whiskers and Battenberg
treats for both

Room with a View (After L.S Lowry, Man Lying on a Wall)

Walking the dog,
minding my own business,
I find this guy lying on a wall.
I doff my cap.
He grunts. I continue on my way.

Next morning, he's there again.
I bid him 'Good Morning'.
He grunts.
My dog cocks his leg.
We continue on our way.

On the third morning
I offer him a butty,
finest cheddar and piccalilli.
He grunts.
My dog pinches his brolly.

Fourth morning, he's not there.
On tiptoes, I peer over the wall.
I see two windows with open curtains,
buxom ladies sit at each.
My dog barks.

On the fifth morning
I climb onto the empty wall.
A man walks by and offers me Costa.
I grunt.
My dog waits at home.

Three Hundred and Sixty-One Degrees

I could write a poem about the Seasons,
how worm casts pepper spring's dew-fed lawns
and pirate gulls swipe cones from tearful kids
as summer evenings recede from sun-filled play.

Why not a poem charged with autumn fire,
about windswept fury dragging twigs
and bulbous pumpkins growing lantern-teeth,
before winter's icicled Swan Lake dance?

My blood-sweat tee shirt has worn thin,
Thesaurus pages are grimed, note-books creak
from razor genius, but my ideas vapourise
before black ink scrolls. Nothing shouts 'Me'.

I could write a poem about me writing a poem,
about the quest for original voice, threads woven
through layers of honey stacked waffles…
Perhaps I'll write another poem about the Seasons…

Entropy and Soap

in perfect sequence   at some specific
angle
        with weasel-fear   I'm all a shiver outside
mathematic   logarithmic   horrific
    I can't abide   my systems crash inside

a piece of soap should be arbitrary
yes
        it's packaged and sold   neat rows in line
but at home   revolutionary   visionary   not
disciplinary
                a skew-whiff soap-dish is entropy-fine

his OCD   symmetry fixation
orthogonal
            to vertical   t   the soap must conform
                            a
                            p

anticipation of no organisation = immobilisation
I surf the wave   to neutralise   the growing storm

I will not   debate   humiliate   or agitate
I will placate   asphyxiate   and cremate

She

(after: Woman with a Fork in a Winter Landscape, 1883 Van Gogh)

She doesn't see the face of cold
nor the age-worn bite of loss
she doesn't hear the silent longing
nor weary rumble of haggard time
she doesn't smell green envy of want
nor sense death's close knock
she doesn't taste fear in earth's deep breath

she sees hope as silky roots burst
and thaw her frost-bit heart
she hears bird-song glitter winter trees
and tell of nests and birthing young
she smells the rise of phloem's promise
and lives the whisper of infinitude
she is a mother who feeds her young
and lives the whisper of infinitude
she smells the rise of phloem's promise
and tells of nests and birthing young
she hears bird-song glitter winter trees
and thaw her frost bit heart
she sees hope as silky roots burst

she doesn't taste fear in earth's deep breath
nor sense death's close knock
she doesn't smell green envy of want
nor weary rumble of haggard time
she doesn't hear the silent longing
nor the age worn bite of loss
she doesn't see the face of cold

Absent Guest (after: Tea in a Bedsitter – Harold Gilman)

It's all blue, blasted blue, the floor,
ceiling, and walls, with bits of red.
Why not yellow and orange
in nightmare swirls?

It's the same routine every Sunday,
Mother lays tea for four
at four pm, on a damask tablecloth
in the spare room.

Father calls it *the Bedsit,*
bed by the wall, chair at the window,
it's his *Arles,* a shrine
in his idol's honour.

Wearing blue, we wait.
Footsteps from his studio creak floorboards,
Father pours, we drink stewed tea.
Vincent's chair remains empty.

Lost Anchor

You are not the 6am shower
following a morning run, after-shave
splashed before double espresso,
a dash in open-toe sandals
and pinstripe to catch the 7.52.
You are not the empty, green leather
office chair nor the unopened mail.

You are the call of hungry gull
diving for pork-pie scraps.
You are stillness of black sea silence
to children's bubbling laughter
as they build sandcastles
with red buckets and spades.
Your atoms wash their paddling feet.

You are the name inked on my inner arm,
 the memory that grounds a mother's tide.

Kaas

(Family Portrait   *Maarteen Van Heemskerck, Germany, 1530)*

Horn honking, taxi waits, clock
ticking pounds; Dad yells to kids
on social media, Jan, aged five,
posts selfies to school buddies,
Cornelia's sticky fingers
stub thumbnails of Grandpops.

Mama carries young Pieter wrapped
in shawl, they'll meet the grand-parents
at the Photographic studio –
been in the family since the sixteenth
century, although it was all oil paints
in those days, rather than digital.

Posing, Jan clutches his iPad,
Cornelia her A.I. doll and Dad,
with earbuds, clings to his laptop
tuned to Bloomberg for the latest FTSE
news. Pieter grabs Mama's silver cross.
On the count of three, the family smile.

In true tradition, a celebration meal
had been booked to bribe the youngsters –
not pies and produce from the region
but BigMacs, Fries and Thickshakes.
The portrait hangs in the Heemskerck gallery.

Defaid, Cawl and Progress

Where grass grows lush green
to a rhythmic grind of sheep jaws
and the timpani tap of the woodpecker;
we don't want the static buzz of pylons.

Where the afon Banwy tickles trout
and kids from Llanfair Primary,
still innocent, play Pooh-sticks;
we don't want road churning trucks.

Where sheep speckle green hillsides
like white stars on a clear Welsh night
and locals stagger home from the *Eirlys*
at midnight, don't give us diggers

and pipelines and rubble dumps
to kill our yellow poppies, wild orchids,
bat habitats and red-belly newts.
Don't wrench our hedgerows

to widen roads, to bring civilisation
to my homeland, where people
still value community, sing Ballads,
Cerdd Dant and leave doors unlocked.

A Brother's Journey

As we sit by the coal fire
I scribble agreed Hymns and Readings
on a scrap of paper,
I add your half-read novel to the Oxfam pile.

I pack your pyjamas and a change of clothes,
into the green canvas bag
you used for Lake District getaways.
Today is different.

Your yellow fag-stained fingers
add photos of Jan before your divorce,
and the kids paddling at Harlech –
fragments of home for bedside comfort.

You don't reproach me for kicking
Mungo's empty dog-food bowl
as you sink your key into the mortice deadlock
and close the chipped, blue-painted gate.

As we drive, leaving the hamlet,
you don't look back.
No music rocks
from your Seventies Collection.

You stand by mud-splattered daffodils
in the car park, black body-warmer
hanging limp off your skeletal form,
bones scarcely camouflaged by flesh.

I could go back

Seventy miles north
on a no-through street
is a nineteenth century
miner's cottage with walls
as thick as memories buried.

Car full of petrol,
my diary empty,
I could pack a picnic,
fill a flask, grab a coat,
and iPhone to capture images.

I could walk those childhood lanes,
smell the chimney smoke,
taste Mrs. Robert's Bara-Brith,
relive the pain of Clive Jones' stones
aimed at my seven-year-old legs.

I could stand at the bottom
of the slate steps
and look up to the verdigris
brass-lion knocker
on a faded scarlet front door.
I could…

Looking Out (after: Cape Cod Morning 1950, Edward Hopper)

She peers to morning's yellow wash of hope,
tractor tyres churn pot-holed lanes,
distant gulls echo the sea.

early sunshine peeps over the Carneddau
to play on greening oak-buds
bursting promise
I know   I don't need confirmation   I know

Her dog sits one ear cocked in ever readiness.
Three years ago, the master left a scribbled note
under the peppermill.
She waits.

part of me
through this glow   this morning kiss
still trumpets hope despite poor prognosis

He will return.
If only she had listened that night.
She carries his words in her core.

I bathe in spring air
and disown pyrites
She breathes autumn gold.

With time our morning rituals
become monotony,
waiting,
for words to leach through letterboxes.

the oncologist's all-clear
today will be the start

Nothing from him,
she peers out to void.

Akureyri

The flight from Birmingham to Reykjavik
was turbulent under thick cloud.
After one night in a hotel with sulfur water,
our spirits further dampened by a depressive

taxi driver, we waited in a shed-like airport
to fly north, to the small, less cosmopolitan
Akureyri. We gazed as snow peaks pierced
clouds below us as the eighty-seater plane

bumped its way to Icelandic chatter
from the loud, local working-folk
taking little notice of intruding travellers
oohing and ahing through ice-crystal windows.

The magic of red-tiled roof-ridges
peering through foot-deep snow,
the clanking of chains on car wheels,
the yells of laughter from drinkers sipping

Brennivín floating on geothermal lagoons
at midnight, the forever Christmas cottage
lit in Santa joy, were but a breath of this haven,
a refuge, a convalescence where sky danced

with green elves and scarlet goblins
to the music of moving tectonic plates,
bubbling pits and devilish basalt pillars.
This land of vastness, of wilderness

where Viking horses roam returning
to their home-valley to die, this land
was where I found strength to fight
to live and not to die.

Les Rêves d'une Poule dans le Jardin

Finished for another day –
he's such a show-off, plumage
neatly combed, head-gear
sparkling red, spiked like a Mohican.
His calls wake the neighbourhood.

Five a.m., I'll grab another forty-winks,
there's time before the human chicks
come carrying a wicker basket
in search of breakfast eggs.
I don't mind, but it is manners to ask.

I know – we wouldn't be kept
if we didn't lay eggs, grain isn't cheap,
we'd be… dare I mention it…
stuffed with sage & onion for the pot!
Who says a cluck-full day is a bed of roses?

Moving to Wales

Let there be light and there isn't,
not in this house. Pendants hang
40W bulbs, sufficient to find the kettle
and brew up a quick cuppa,
poor enough to hide the mounting dust.

Sockets... one per room
not where you need them – OK
for the tele and a 60's two-bar fire,
as there's no central heating.

Hubby's well chuffed, Amazon
rules, parcel after parcel, the postman
sighs – it's a way up the potholed lane.

Switches, bulbs, light fittings,
extension leads, drills for ancient
three-foot stone walls... 'you'll go halves
won't you Darling?' I smile and nod.

As I feared – dust is now visible,
so, I christen the sockets
with a quick whip round with the hoover,
before fish and chips
in-front of the log fire.

Kill to Eat

Early hours before sun stretches
across the garden, I glance
through open window, larch trees sway
to morning breeze. A mewing call,

dark tipped wings swoop, a buzzard's
razor yellow talons lift a rabbit.
I watch black and white under-wings

span in flight, such strength. I shudder
at the rabbit's demise,
the cruelty of nature, the natural cycle.

Now, wide awake, slippered feet
go downstairs to the kettle.
In the corner, behind the bin
I see the mousetrap has caught its prey.

What I See

Leggy 11, mirror's cruel truth -
Look at your acne.
Squashing black-heads
is fun, but leaves red marks
where fingers bruise the skin.
A rub of talc conceals.

Shock-em 17, to rock not clock,
is the lippy straight,
mascara black enough?
You'll make your parents tut tut.
I want mysterious not full-goth,
but sexier than Liz next-door

 Flowering 22, open window rose scent
lifts clouds. Mirror's buffed a shine
for my Summer wedding dress,
crisp swan-white and borrowed blue.
Your Angel wings step centre-stage.

Caged 44, kitchen, kids and ketchup,
eye-bag scowls through mirror dust,
and wrinkles nudge from smile lines.
That moisturiser will do no good.
I hang ironing over the mirror.

Grandma 65, cream-cake
waistline, a plump face hides
my concertina neck.
'Hey*!*' I banish the mirror
to inner wardrobe door.

Sofa 70, warm contentment,
a forgotten face stares back,
a bubbling smile, laughing eyes,
life's fullness reflects.
Now she sees my ornate frame.

I Throw the Dice…

Like batting a shuttle cock across the net,
words climb ladders and slither
down. It's all one big deal to trump
the opposition as sticks bully-off
on winter's pitch. Ice crystals sparkle
but melt in anger's fire as jokers rule.

Pack wolves yowl and chew,
battleships approach aiming high to my mask.
I scrabble tiles, letters fall clank
like slates from a roof,
spelling nothing, a checkered diagonal,
black draughts through wood-rot windows,
curtains heavy, it's checkmate.

I am ready
to pass through red velvet
as organ pipes resonate,
no more passing Go
no two-hundred pounds.
They ask:
'You OK?'
'Yes', I say.
Alpha to omega,
I feed the hangman's blanks.

Father

This is a poem
not about…

… stale dust on photograph frames,
pine air-fresheners
camouflaging age's soiled bedlinen
under youth's faded floral-eiderdown.

… the For Sale board
and red-taped boxes packed to the roof,
as I drive the grass-ribboned mountain lane,
from your cottage, caught piws by evening sun.

Is it about that December evening,
when shops blasted Frosty and Jingle Bells,
and a white van went through on red
stealing your winter?   No…

It is the touch of skin, cheek to cheek
our noses rubbing to my girly giggles,
and how the size of your curling hand,
engulfed my daisy-chain fingers.

Distillation to Anhydrous Product

Her bait – obsidian eyes,
promises of phosphorous fire,
a mouth curled moue
latent in soignée decorum.

My path's unclear, catalysed
by aqueous sulphuric acid,
gentle reflux, toluene nitrated,
gives a gunpowder reaction.

I step barefoot on the parquet floor,
my cayenne thermostat off scale,
with cavernous hunger,
towards her coy, simmering Zambra.

Dressed, crystalline punch
in prismatic colour, she peers,
a giggle, her tongue orthogonal.
My taper's lit, I stare mesmerised.

Daylight fleeting shadows
whip pyrites to emptiness.
Diamond dreams allotrope
to a graphite reality.

I dance

I dance barefoot
to June's mad, hypnotic rhythm
in meadows of wild flowers.

War-red poppies talk man's
thirst for blood,
unending in modern days.

The boundary fragile,
new alliances between nations
are thinner than filo.

Sky-blue cornflowers
catalyse aspirations,
teaching higher values.

Few learn.
Suspicion reigns in man's kingdom.
Good intentions are short lived.
I dance free as the blackbird.

Insomnia

Sleep eludes
my tangled mind.
Insomnia grips
like a coffin, snug, this barren night.

Awake – my dreams are cast away
on the Mary Rose,
my sheets are sails trapping thoughts
in woven webs.
I pitch on open deck,
relentless.
No peace is found below the mocking stars.

Hours blend to haze.
I listen for grandfather-clock chimes,
timpani beats that resonate my ear.
Morpheus fails to take my hand
and lead me to slumber's shore.

Tea,
a read,
a blank page,
words churn like stomach acid,
a spark ignites, the taper's lit,
syllables and feet run across in lines.
In the owl-hoot black,
no counting the stars.
I laugh and outstare sleep.

As night resolves towards the crimson hour,
a free man released from prison bars,
I kiss insomnia.

Scrambled eggs,
a TV nap,
clean mugs in a line,
a new packet of Bourbons
ready — I must sharpen tonight's pencils.
Le Fin.

Yoke of Man

eggs
elegant ovoids
eggsactly what's needed
eggcellent source of protein
eggsperiment with the cooking
eggspanding your techniques
eggstracting the fullest flavour
eggsample fry boil or poach
elaborate eggs Benedict
eggspensive   no cheap
eggsuberantly yellow
eggciting the taste
eggstolling the
eggsential
egg

Rain Dance

They look up to the sky,
a crowd of sepia people
immune to neck ache.
They watch and wait,

silence punctuated by wings
flapping, heading south searching.
A child cries but the mother
holds tight, she keeps her pose

looking and praying
as yet another day passes unblessed.
Their crops lie shrivelled, no grain
to barter, no food for man or beast.

The raindancer, frenetic, his matted curls
and arms cutting air faster than focus,
dances to mother earth's rhythm,
bellowing her call to Lord Indra.

Others rest, sleepless on barren dust
under a cloudless sky
to echoes of forest animals
howling at dry watering-holes.

(Lord Indra — Hindu God of rain)

Confirmation Day Promises

(after 'The Arrival of Spring at Holgate – Hockney)

To be a bride is a future dream
but Mum says this is the next best thing.
My white dress, delicately crafted
by Grandma, hangs over my bedroom
door. It was Mum's before mine
and she's a good Christian lady.

I finger the scar of ridged bodice-stitches.
Ben, our sheepdog, clawed a tear
chasing rabbits in meadow blossom sleep.
Mother's late-night embroidery conceals
the rip with strawberry-ice rosebuds –
but I know it is there.

I play with the frilly under-layers,
wondering whether God will mind
if I wear my favourite pink knickers
underneath. I told him, on my knees
last night, it was for confidence, to feel
as pretty as the girls wearing new dresses.

Mary Simpson's Jubilee

No-one's celebratin me, my 70 years of service,
I'm up each mornin wi t'lark settin tables an scrubbin sink,
fryin bacon, straight from fatted pig. The smell in my hair
is bad for likes of me – vegetarian. I don't go wi them
that kills flesh to eat, nor wi them that call it sport,
all ponced-up in tweeds wi a tally-ho an hounds
barkin across t'valley an settin off farm dogs.

No-one's celebratin me, my 70 years' service,
I'm up each mornin on my knees, being thankful
wi prayers for them's that's not bothered,
that takes it as their birth-right to have health
and money to fritter wi 'out knowin worth of nought.
I don't go wi costly clutter when there's folk
homeless and starvin in war and drought-dry lands.

No-one's celebratin me, my 70 years of service
to family, neighbours, community, Queen and planet,
as I plant a tree in my back yard and remember t'day
70 years ago – I stood on t'corner of street
wi Mam and Auntie Dot. We was wavin Coronation flags
promisin to serve our Queen.

But for flick of butterfly wing, that could be me –
Mary Simpson, spinster of Parish celebratin
my Platinum Jubilee. No hard feelins your Majesty.
I give thanks and raise my glass of stout to the tele –
Salt of the earth, God Bless you Ma'am.

Bathed

I trundle through forests of dark mire,
stumbling on knots of moss-clad roots,
to an oasis of lime green, lit by rising moon.

There stands a peacock, solitary,
plumage tight against his body.

Stretching tall,

he fans his cobalt finery
adorned with jade and ultramarine.

Our eyes merge.

The yoke of yesterday's fog lifts.
The valley below dawns
as I pick up the discarded feather.

Peacock is a Christian symbol of eternal life; its tough skin doesn't decay
quickly after death. Circles on feathers represent the eyes of God. Feathers
fall out and regrow... eternal life.

Thermostat Set Low

Cattle shelter in warmth of barns,
fields squelch to my walking-boots,

blue and coal tits squabble for peanuts.
In wool fleece and thermal slippers,

I weigh out fruits and spices,
fresh flour and muscovado sugar,

mixing in butter and farm-fresh eggs.
The cake, infused with brandy

is stored in eco-unfriendly foil.
Squirrels dig for acorn stores,

snowdrops force through frozen earth.
No family offer me help to peel and scrape,

their fingers dance on gadgets
to blaring TV background.

*'Sorry Darling. Got to pop out,
got to buy your present.'*

That man thing, Christmas Eve:
'Couldn't find anything practical

I'll treat you in the January Sales.
Come the big day, they burp and snore,

I take a walk on my own.
Sheep graze as yesterday,

blackbirds serenade,
coal-tits still feed on peanuts.

Not a white Christmas,
just anticyclonic gloom.

His Song

1

This isn't about where I'm sitting
with its vaulted ceiling,
old oak doors enclosed behind glass,
matt-black Swedish log-burner
with stainless steel chimney
exhaling waste gases to the outside.

Having set up my easel,
chosen my palette,
it is about the colour of solitude
and safety to paint my own space.

2

It is not about winter-magnified cold,
church pillars encroaching,
black-suited sleeves diffusing
to goose-pimpled hands
as they hold the *Order of Service.*
It's not about *all things bright and beautiful.*

Having buried my brother
It's now about loss of order,
squashed time,
it's about, why is he dead at 56?

3

It's not about tantalised tastebuds,
lobster goujons with courgette fries,
and champagne bubbles, nor is at about
the wake's curl-crust sandwiches,
pies and beer, nor the cackle
of – *ad-too-many- alves* Aunt Olive.

Having tasted the earth,
his sweet nature and lemon-tang humour,
it is the ashes to ashes return.
I am left with fresh air, absence, void.

4

It's not about his rattle-tin-van,
axle whining on each pothole.
It isn't about radio 2, ABBA and 80's scene,
nor his voice of Plaid Cymru
against my apathy. Nor is it the toll
of Rizla papers and strike of that final match.

Gone are those fag-stained fingers,
and gurgling slate-rumble cough.
Having meditated his silence –
It's the yell – I miss his cheery lilt.

Life is a Cup of Tea

That first sip quenches thirst
like snowflakes tickling the happiness
of laughter's youth… the perfect Yorkshire brew.

Ginger and Ginseng, passion-fire from the east,
bodies entwined on sunbaked cicada nights
 a vortex of spiralling tornado unleashed.

Darjeeling, elegance of forgotten courtship
dances, waltzing the herringbone floors.
Tomorrows line up, bone-china waiting to break.

Green leaves, a surge of sap
invigorates blood to navigate arteries
like long-boats voyaging a series of locks.

Ceylon, or should it be Sri-Lankan,
decades have flown on hummingbird wing.
Perfect tea for a slice of lemon.

Brown leaves stewed by autumn's winds
brush immortality with graveyard shadow
as arthritis bites like a lobster claw.

Broken teabags, a caddy of stale dust,
can be buried as fertiliser, good for roses
and remembrance lawns.

Distant Voices
(after 'Memories of Christmas' Dylan Thomas)

We tobogganed down the hill,
towards the Welsh-speaking sea,
like a moon bundling down the sky.

At the ice-edge, fish-freezing waves,
it was snowing, white as Lapland,
though no reindeer. We snowballed cats

and padded streets leaving spoon-footprints.
'What would you do if I saw a hippo?'
'I'd raise my arm, go bang and eat snow-pie.'

'Can fish see through sea and see it's snowing?'
'They think the sky's falling down.'
Trudging desolate streets homeward,

we stumbled on ancient oak roots
in mine-soot black, to the cries of ghosts
carrying their heads underarm.

Kraken and Yeti lurked in shadows
of fear, '*Once in Royal*?'
'No, *Come All Ye Faithful*.'

'I'll count to three.'
We sang fortissimo in toy-soprano.
Earth-dry voices added bass harmony.

Quantum Field Thicket

In the quiet quark of twilight,
when photons exchange
at low intensity, a fox,
mindful of its wavelength,
drifts through a neutrino forest,
diffracting through tree gaps,
as tight circular waves.

After tankards of Heineken,
Herr Heisenberg observes
with definite uncertainty –
he cannot concurrently compute
the exact location and speed
of that red bushy tail.
Is it quantum or particle
or a case of duality?

Strolling through the muon mist
near Hadrian's wall,
he chats with Hadron,
a composite,
two quarks better than one.
The advice given is: *keep low,*
hide from Wizard Lepton.

If Lepton should flick his wand,
a photon sea would cast a spell:
All creatures within projectile range
would sleep for eons
unless kissed by a charm.
What is the probability of maidens fair
traversing these parts on such a night?

Tonight

As winter's lion roars through dark of night,
I dream your arms wrap me warm, in hold, tonight.

You don't come dancing to my rose-clad porch,
nor whistle mermaid songs to moon's bold night.

Your haunting shadow flits grey cirrus cloud,
 you jig and jive, life's origami folds to night.

Heavy curtains, citric tears of despair,
your smile's a mask, your absent heart cold to night.

Alone, I read your letters, poetic nonsense –
you paint us travelling rainbows to golden night.

I hear silence, your vacant eyes speak no time.
Me, I will not cross your threshold late tonight.

**To the Butterfly who flapped wings, and my thanks
and Season's greetings to...**

the Fiat driver who splashed
my white trousers causing delay,
the taxi driver who took the wrong turn,
the jeweller who closed his shop on time
so I couldn't' buy a diamond ring,

the restaurateur who had sold out
of Champagne, the good phone signal
for Charlotte to dump me, the thief who lifted
my wallet at the urinal, to the fake Santa

with his *Ho Ho Ho* that lit the face
of the policewoman, Ann, who listened
to my tale of woe and invited me home
for pizza, and later became my wife.
Sincerely yours, Happy from Hertford.

The Slow Road Circumventing the Wrekin

My task is to write a poem as a sort
of stream of consciousness, but
edit it to give a picture which starts
then goes off at right-angles to radius
before coming back in a grand finale
loop, as though planted like tubers –
but not. That's all very well for experts,
people like Billy Collins and Robert Frost,
but here's looking at me.

I fumble around stirring words,
grabbing snippets of ideas as they float past
on someone else's pea-green boat.
I'm given a few hints, not totally alone
in the Sahara Desert with just wiggly
snakes riffing patterns in golden sand,
as they sideways walk with more panache
than my feet – two steps up, one slide down.

Back to the guidelines; I can give
the Who? Where? When? Why? What? –
Great how all those words begin with W.
Maybe I'll add an intruder – an 'If.'
If I tiptoe clouds above the mundane,
anywhere, anywhen, anywho, anywhat –
I'll float to my yesterdays neatly filed
by emotion red, blue, green, yellow,
purple, to the pinnacle, to the Eiffel Tower.
Tomorrows are out of reach, strictly confidential,
chained and padlocked, their labels left blank.

I'm playing, I'm not getting on with the serious,
no – never serious, business of poetry.
Poetry is life in words, it's when
you leave the staid, the oh so po-faced,
and let truth peep out. It's those moments
when another's fingertips touch your truth.

So, here I am, armed
with keyboard and screen ready to tell you –
the who… that's me, the where… that's here,
the when… that's now –
                                but I'll leave you
as I ponder, with Yorkshire strong brewed tea,
the What… that unknown, the 'x'
in simultaneous equations yet to be solved.

Vita Poetica

To write
a poem that's
unique to me, not like
ones done before is difficult
to do.

To do
a syllabic
piece, finding rhythmical
words which carry my voice in truth
takes time.

Take time
to strive and sing
from sheer delight beyond
mere mortal sight; a poet sees
from heart.

From heart
to throat – I pour
another cup of tea
procrastination, blank pages
no words.

No words,
ears deaf, no muse
to guide the spirit's flow,
flask empty, pencil sharp, I wait
to write.

The Grass is Finer

Come shepherd, sit a while
where time has stopped in hills
carved by volcanoes singing
the ancient Occitan tongue.
The river foams, twisting to forgotten
words that roamed brackened fell
under blue skies of the Auvergne.

Come, escape drum-beat toil,
leave hum-drum chores behind,
let your eyes rest and swirl
in nature's swelling buds
by the stream you dare not cross.

Your flock has gone to browner land,
to promises of measured nutrient feed,
devoid of earth's wild taste.
Stay with the ancient oaks, Balïèro,
breathe meadow sweet land.
The bridge is here, come sit with me.

(Inspired by: Canteloube – 'Balïèro')

Cotton Fields

It's a barren night on the midnight fell,
owl and nightingale sit low in fear,
ice-air bites and frog-eyes swell.

A rush of wind tears leaves with dragon's spear,
head-voices rise in incandescent screech,
tomorrow's shadow hovers ever near.

On my knees, arms outstretched in prayer, I reach
in vain to wedding promises you made –
empty as dove-silk feathers doused in bleach.

Moon's cotton whispers through the yew tree shade —
'Go home, where sunshine lifts and rainbows fall,
where tide and time washed memories will fade.'

I listen to a lapwing's plaintive call
rising from its earth-nest to heaven's light,
my breath diffuses through the arrow-slit wall.

Prologue complete, a new page open, white
cotton ginned, carded, spun, wound and finished,
I see the natural flow of life in flight.

Morning curtains open, mist diminished,
my soul skips through the meadow, replenished.

Where the Elephant Sings

To know what animals know –
I'll go down to where the elephant sings.

I'll catch the slow bus past the privet,
past Aldi, pausing at the zebra crossing
where cars hoot at striped heads swaying
from left to right taking no notice
of red-faced businessmen shaking fists.
A zebra is always crossing, never crossed.

I'll leave angry bus passengers
and stroll beyond the cuckoo call
to where the elephant thumples dusty paths,
immune to pheasant goodnight frenzies,
his trunk a metronome to rhythm of Bach.

I'll sit in the dark, utterly free,
on dew-swept grass and listen
to his trumpet solo, a rallentando
to fading light, before the final cadence.

Crystal Gardens

Wear goggles, pour 3cm of corrosive
sodium silicate into a beaker, add hot water
to a depth of 12cm, stir with a glass rod
until the solution shows no separate layers.

Read the Cleapss Hazard cards
for all substances used. Add blue cobalt,
red-brown iron, and green nickel sparingly,
(its compounds are potential carcinogens).
White magnesium salts give a stark,
ghostly background of twiggy growth,
and manganese offers pink rose buds.

Overnight the garden will grow,
as the coloured silicates precipitate.
Added snippets of twig and holly leaf
give an authentic scene –
a crystal garden like shreds of glass.

Broken glass, crystal splinters
littered streets as synagogues burnt –
a reality precipitated from Nazi hatred.
Stark, no Hazard cards available .

The world changed that night,
9th November,1938.
Crystal gardens grew blood red
from a corrosive final solution.
Goggles offered no protection.

The People I didn't know

She wasn't there.
She had gone,
but we didn't know where.
We didn't know.
She had taken her stuff
and my little brother, Tom.
She wasn't there.

Father searched.
There was no note.
The neighbours knew,
but wouldn't say.
She wasn't there.

I don't know what happened next,
except we talked, and talked…
Father, my two older brothers
and I sat round the kitchen table
with endless cups of tea.
It made us kids feel important.
We'd never talked like this before.

I heard Father on the telephone –
angry one moment,
pleading the next.
I guessed he was talking to Mother.
I heard him crying at night.

She didn't come back.
They lived in Wokingham, but –
there were no letters, birthday cards
or Christmas presents.

Twelve years later,
when I was eighteen, I caught a train.
When I saw them again,
they were strangers.

Do you know?

What's wrong with knowing what you know now
and not knowing what you don't know until later?
Knowledge is a fickle game, high-brow, holy-cow.
What's wrong? With knowing what you know now
as truth, leave catty lies buried in furrows – Meow!
Gossip is a not-knowing disease of human nature –
that's what's wrong with knowing what you know now
and not knowing what you don't know until later.

*What's wrong with knowing what you know now and not knowing
what you don't know now until later?" A.A Milne*

Iceland

On arrival, I peer through Akureyri's grey, snow-filled sky;
red roof tiles cheer the months of continuous freeze and short
daylight hours. Icelandic sheep wool, with an extra 'pel' layer,
offers insulation against sub-zero temperatures.

> Feet trudge through deep snow,
>   red roof-tiles grow icicles,
>   hands thaw in wool gloves.

On our second day, we wake to six feet of snow. An army of
ploughs, chained wheels higher than my head, with large
baskets, push and raise snow onto lorries. We watch as load
after load is emptied into the sea, floating like icebergs on the
blue-grey ripple. Locals continue daily life unperturbed.

> Red hats, orange ploughs,
>   wheel-chains grind ice to crystals.
>   Buds bulge on bare trees.

On a jeep excursion, skidding on virgin snow and compacted
ice, over boulders, at stomach-moving angles; we are taken
off-road to a giant horseshoe-shaped canyon, just north of
Dettifoss. It is said to be left by Sleipnir, the eight-legged
horse of the Norse god Odin. Others believe it was caused by
floods when glaciers burst. We look down hundreds of feet at
ice carvings, as waterfalls power and freeze en route to the
steel-blue lake at the canyon head.

Close by, people in bathing costumes lie in hot springs.
Glasses clink as they drink Brennivin to the sulphurous gurgle
and phut of geysers.

Thunderous bellows,
waterfalls carve ice statues,
Steam heats Myvatn lake.

To see the northern lights against clear skies has been a
lifelong desire. Wrapped in thermal merino- wool layers,
against the -25 degrees centigrade, we are taken by minibus to
the first location – no joy, second location – the slightest hint
of zig-zag green.
   'We'll try one further place.' says the driver. One mile down
the road… the Sky-Elves dance… red, green ghost
shimmering waves. Cameras click, incessant to the Prima
Donna's tune.

Sky dance, green whisper,
pulsing curtain against black
caught on camera.

Souvenirs – thick hand-knitted gloves and fair-isle sweaters
with colour-patterned yokes, hang in moth proof bags.
   I pack the maps away on the travel bookshelf, along with
the Teach Yourself Icelandic discs and phrase books, with
promises to revisit, to rekindle the candle-glow, the warmth of
our welcome.
   Will those embers die as the clothes' moth finds his way?

Barren to bustle,
maps and fairisle packed away.
Clothes' moth finds his feast.

Of Cabbages, Soup and Software

I woke this morning fretting –
cabbages   red cabbages
should have been harvested last year...
then... there's carrots and parsnips
sweating in the fridge, waiting
as pumpkins hibernate
until I'm organised to make soup...

but I must create book cover designs...
with new Affinity software,
manual's coming today, from Amazon.
I fear gobbledegook instructions,
instructions...
bleed and gutter margins
            page size...   what about the food shop?

We're out of butter and down to a handful of teabags.
Enough petrol? The nearest shop is five miles.
Those pumpkins sit heavy...
Instructions all about RGB, shapes, filters,
        drag and drop
                    red cabbages with slug eaten holes
    iPad 2% charged
                    carrots gone black

I'll go for the butter   click to template
      and   plant broad beans this afternoon
new season's underway   cabbages   Times Roman 12
    butter   save to pdf   pumpkins
        slugs   red cabbages
                gobbledegook
          soup   RGB
          get more carrots
                petrol gauge low …
                    energy gauge
                            low
                              e
                              r

Dancing Shoes

Pink with long ties
to go round my ankles
and hard toes
to support en pointe,
I twirled in pirouette.

I kept them at the back
of my shoe cupboard,
behind outgrown slippers,
and school uniform
hot weather sandals.

At night I'd open
my most precious book,
Grandma's gift
costing 21 shillings.
The pictures

in the book were all of me;
the tutus soft frilly pink,
my long hair tied in a bun
on top of my head.

I'd grown a bit
and practiced a lot
but the pages show
me on stages across the world,
people throwing pink roses
as I curtsy… they clap
until their claps are used up…

they didn't say I was too tall,
they didn't say I had no balance
or not enough money for lessons,
they didn't say I was a liar,
and that there were no shoes
with pink ribbons to tie round my ankles.

They didn't tell me...

I didn't watch the King's Christmas
message to his loyal subjects,
instead, I folded wrapping-paper
ready to use it again.

When my sons spoke in whispers.
I thought it impolite,
but gave them cake and wished
them a Happy New Year.

Strong men carried out furniture;
they took coins from under my bed.
I made them coffee,
but forgot their two sugars.

Seat belted, rug over my knees,
I smiled and watched the trees
pass at speed.
I hadn't been to Rose Cottage before.

A lady with a cheery smile
welcomed me on the doorstep.
I didn't know then...
I wouldn't be going back home.

Four Sat Round the Kitchen Table...

Four eggs in different coloured foils –
blue, red, green and yellow, sit
in Beatrix Potter cups, wrapped
with saucers, in ribboned cellophane.

Tony methodically unwraps the red.
He munches slowly with purpose,
three-quarters neatly returned
to the cup nest for tomorrow.

Alasdair tears green aluminium,
teeth bite chocolate apex, crisscross
pattern crumbles. Eaten within the hour,
wrapping scrunched by a satisfied hand.

Charles watches and mimics his brothers,
pulling at yellow foil, chocolate lipstick
smeared round his two-year old gurgle smile.
Mother controls his intake – don't want indigestion.

I look at my blue egg, I'll keep that for later.
I'm more interested in the story
on the cup and saucer. I want to explore
with Peter Rabbit in Mr. McGregor's Garden.

Dear Santa

Early settlement would be appreciated.
I enclose an itemised statement
of brand and price inclusive of VAT,
for each present I bought for our four children,
Samantha, Thomas, James and Charlotte,
from birth to eighteen, which is the accepted age
of adulthood. I feel this is fair as you have failed
to respond to all correspondence over the years,
where I have cited evidence of each child's
consistent good behaviour, and enumerated
their non-extravagant present requests.

Consequently, I seek reimbursement.
The monies owed, together with interest
in accordance with current inflation rates,
have mounted.
Please contact me, by email,
for banking payment details.
Failure to comply may result in legal proceedings.

My Boy

I bought an offcut of fur
from Russian artists at Hugglets –
barely enough for head and arms

with double-espresso   glasses
and eager-nerves   I cut
metal pin-joints with clippers

threadbare segments soak
in baby-soft shampoo –
much less than the sum of parts

precision   thread and needle
I pin lining material   each stitch
is crafted with decades of respect

perished bellows   his voice-box
silenced   I oil and seal
to rekindle a phoenix growl

wood-wool stuffed extremities
amber eyes catch morning sun
vintage ears no longer floppy

eighteen inches of red ribbon
I tie a bow with pride
under his embroidered smile.

Lost Carnation of Andalucia

Seasoned by years, I meander
through Eastern markets,
a kaleidoscopic maze of silks and spices –

turmeric, saffron and sage.
Snakes uncoil and rise to a haunting
flute. I rewind to our cicada

nights, when your coal-black eyes flashed
and your red dress flicked with rhythm
to the wail and stamp of Flamenco.

Latin fire sparked to the clap of castanets,
flooding blood through youthful veins;
that night, our hunger danced to a crescendo.

Now, I lean on a crooked cane and capture
digital memories for grandchildren. Inside
I still ache for your flame.

Thank you for reading

Coloured Truths

Francesca Hunt

Notes

Milton Keynes UK
Ingram Content Group UK Ltd.
UKHW021604100924
448141UK00013B/599

9 781445 759616